Will Carleton

Young folks' centennial rhymes

Will Carleton

Young folks' centennial rhymes

ISBN/EAN: 9783743328532

Manufactured in Europe, USA, Canada, Australia, Japa

Cover: Foto ©ninafisch / pixelio.de

Manufactured and distributed by brebook publishing software (www.brebook.com)

Will Carleton

Young folks' centennial rhymes

CONTENTS.

	PAGE
THE LITTLE BLACK-EYED REBEL	19
THE BOSTON BOYS	24
THE FAITHFUL SISTER	30
THE RIDE OF JENNIE M'NEAL	35
THREE SCENES OF A HERO'S LIFE	45
THE PARENTS' FAREWELL	62
HOW ISRAEL WAS WHIPPED	69
LITTLE GOLDEN-HAIR	77
THE PRIZE OF THE "MARGARETTA"	81
THE PRINTER-BOY TRAMP	86
NELLIE'S LIE	89
DICEY LANGSTON	94
NOTES	113

ILLUSTRATIONS.

	PAGE
THE PRIZE OF THE "MARGARETTA"	*Frontispiece*
"WAS WATCHING FOR HIS COMING FROM THE CORNER OF HER EYE"	20
"CLINGING ROUND HIS BRAWNY NECK, SHE CLASPED HER FINGERS WHITE AND SMALL"	23
"THE GENERAL GAZED AT THE FLUSHED FACE RAISED TO HIS, WITH A PLEASED SURPRISE"	28
"'YOU NEVER SHALL KILL THIS BROTHER TILL I HAVE NO HAND TO SAVE'"	32
"SO INTO THE NIGHT THE GRAY HORSE STRODE"	39
"'SINCE YOU HAVE LEFT IT UNTO ME, THUS TO DECIDE I'M LED'"	48
"'WEEP NOT, MY MORE THAN MOTHER; WASTE NOT A SINGLE TEAR'"	56
"JUST BEFORE HIS STEED'S HIGH HEAD, CLAD IN ROBES OF PUREST WHITE"	59
THE PARENTS' FAREWELL	63
"SHE BOUND HIS ARM"	91

YOUNG FOLKS' CENTENNIAL RHYMES.

THE LITTLE BLACK-EYED REBEL.[1]

A BOY drove into the city, his wagon loaded down
With food to feed the people of the British-governed town;
And the little black-eyed rebel, so innocent and sly,
Was watching for his coming from the corner of her eye.

His face looked broad and honest, his hands were brown and tough,
The clothes he wore upon him were homespun, coarse, and rough;
But one there was who watched him, who long time lingered nigh,
And cast at him sweet glances from the corner of her eye.

He drove up to the market, he waited in the line;
His apples and potatoes were fresh and fair and fine;
But long and long he waited, and no one came to buy,
Save the black-eyed rebel, watching from the corner of her eye.

"WAS WATCHING FOR HIS COMING FROM THE CORNER OF HER EYE."

"Now who will buy my apples?" he shouted, long and loud;
And "Who wants my potatoes?" he repeated to the crowd;
But from all the people round him came no word of a reply,
Save the black-eyed rebel, answering from the corner of her eye.

For she knew that 'neath the lining of the coat he wore that day,
Were long letters from the husbands and the fathers far away,
Who were fighting for the freedom that they meant to gain or die;
And a tear like silver glistened in the corner of her eye.

But the treasures — how to get them? crept the question through her mind,
Since keen enemies were watching for what prizes they might find:
And she paused a while and pondered, with a pretty little sigh;
Then resolve crept through her features, and a shrewdness fired her eye.

So she resolutely walked up to the wagon old and red;
"May I have a dozen apples for a kiss?" she sweetly said:
And the brown face flushed to scarlet; for the boy was somewhat shy,
And he saw her laughing at him from the corner of her eye.

"You may have them all for nothing, and more, if you want,"
quoth he.
"I will have them, my good fellow, but can pay for them,"
said she;
And she clambered on the wagon, minding not who all were
by,
With a laugh of reckless romping in the corner of her eye.

Clinging round his brawny neck, she clasped her fingers
white and small,
And then whispered, "Quick! the letters! thrust them un-
derneath my shawl!
Carry back again *this* package, and be sure that you are
spry!"
And she sweetly smiled upon him from the corner of her eye.

Loud the motley crowd were laughing at the strange, un-
girlish freak,
And the boy was scared and panting, and so dashed he
could not speak;
And, "Miss, *I* have good apples," a bolder lad did cry;
But she answered, "No, I thank you," from the corner of
her eye.

"CLINGING ROUND HIS BRAWNY NECK, SHE CLASPED HER FINGERS WHITE AND SMALL."

With the news of loved ones absent to the dear friends they
    would greet,
Searching them who hungered for them, swift she glided
    through the street.
"There is nothing worth the doing that it does not pay to try,"
Thought the little black-eyed rebel, with a twinkle in her eye.

THE BOSTON BOYS.

The General's[2] room had a look of gloom,
    His face bore a deep-marked frown;
With wrinkled brow he was pondering how
    To govern Boston town.

He thought of the care he was doomed to bear
    From the rebels, night and day,
And longed once more to be on the shore
    Of England, far away.

He mused of the trials and self-denials
    That manhood's days annoy,
And wished he could play now and then a day,
    A jolly and careless boy.

Forgetting, though small the troubles all
    Of a child, from manhood's view,
'Tis easily shown, if the truth be known,
    Boys have their troubles, too.

Now the sentinel cried, in the street outside,
  "You bold young rebels, go!"
And the words came loud, as from a crowd,
  "When we do, please let us know!"

"We've a word to say to your chief to-day,"
  Cried a clear voice, young of age:
"You may as well know we never'll go
  Till we've talked with General Gage."

Still the sentinel cried, in the street outside,
  "Begone, you rascally crew!"
The answer sounded, and far resounded,
  "Please hold your breath till we do!"

The General eyed the aid by his side,
  And said, "You had best go out
And view the boys who are making this noise,
  And what it is all about."

And the aid-de-camp, with soldierly tramp,
  Went, looking sober and sage;

But, with a smile on his face the while,
    Came back to General Gage.

"There's a sight to see in the street," said he:
    "Boys a hundred, more or less;
And still they stay, and still they say
    They've a grievance for redress.

"And some have a trace of rage in their face,
    And some a smile to win;
And some are dressed in the city's best,
    And some clad ragged and thin."

The General smiled, for *he* had a child,
    With many a winning way;
And he said, "'Twere no sin; let their leaders in,
    And hear what they have to say."

So eight or ten, like gentlemen,
    Each one with cap in hand,
Marched in and bowed to the General proud,
    And the General's smile was bland.

Then the leader did say, "We have come to-day,
   As of right it doth belong,
To tell you how you should not allow
   Your soldiers to do us wrong.

"Once, twice, and thrice they have broke the ice
   Of our favorite skating-pond;
For naught it was done but to spoil the fun
   Of which we as boys are fond.

"We spoke with them oft, in language soft;
   They only used us worse.
We threatened to see the powers that be;
   They answered us with a curse.

"And we come and say to you to-day,
   Boys have rights as well as men;
This is a free land, and we will not stand
   The breaking our ice again!"

The General gazed at the flushed face raised
   To his, with a pleased surprise;

And the courage-flame that is ever the same
   Sprung into his kindled eyes.

"THE GENERAL GAZED AT THE FLUSHED FACE RAISED
TO HIS, WITH A PLEASED SURPRISE."

He turned to the aid, and softly said,
   "We never can laurels wreathe,

By fighting the ones whose very sons
   Draw liberty when they breathe.

"My lads, you may go; skate to and fro
   In your daily sports once more.
If to spoil your peace they do not cease,
   I will punish my soldiers sore.

"British boys true in spirit are you,
   Whatever may befall."
But they raised a shout, marching briskly out,
   "No! no! we are *Yankees* all!"

THE FAITHFUL SISTER.

Up through the Mohawk Valley, one early morning of May,
The Tories came, with ball and flame, and plundered all the way.

And Samson Sammons' cottage escaped not their regard,'
But safely he and his strong sons three were quick put under guard.

"Now ready, Samson Sammons, you and your strong sons three,"
A soldier said, "My old gray head, and go along with me.

"We must up and off for Canada; we've not a minute to lose."
Said the youngest, "No, I will not go till I've covered my feet with shoes."

"YOU NEVER SHALL KILL THIS BROTHER TILL I HAVE NO HAND TO SAVE!"

"We wait for you not a minute," the cruel soldier said:
"Rebel, go as you are, with your false feet bare, or stay with
 your heart's blood shed."

And the soldier raised his bayonet, to do as he did
 say;
For the boy had sprung for a ladder-rung, determined to
 have his way.

But his faithful, favorite sister, waiting to hear no more,
Undaunted one, sprung on the gun, and pressed it to the
 floor;

And shouted, "Burn and plunder, ye Tories, strong and
 brave!
You never shall kill this brother till I have no hand to
 save!"

For a second's time she struggled to keep her desperate
 clasp;
But with teeth firm clenched, the stout man wrenched his
 gun from the maiden's grasp.

Again he raised the musket, with death to close the strife;
But the chief said, "Stay; she shall have her way: she has earned her brother's life."

And many a bright year after, when war had had its day,
Children there were who petted her, caressing her locks of gray,

And blessed her for the courage with which her love was rife,
Which made its way and gained the day, and saved their father's life.

THE RIDE OF JENNIE M'NEAL.

PAUL REVERE⁴ was a rider bold—
Well has his valorous deed been told;
Sheridan's ride⁵ was a glorious one—
Often it has been dwelt upon.
But why should men do all the deeds
On which the love of a patriot feeds?
Hearken to me, while I reveal
The dashing ride of Jennie M'Neal.

On a spot as pretty as might be found
In the dangerous length of the Neutral Ground,
In a cottage, cozy, and all their own,
She and her mother lived alone.
Safe were the two, with their frugal store,
From all of the many who passed their door;

For Jennie's mother was strange to fears,
And Jennie was large for fifteen years;
With vim her eyes were glistening,
Her hair was the hue of a blackbird's wing;
And while the friends who knew her well
The sweetness of her heart could tell,
A gun that hung on the kitchen wall,
Looked solemnly quick to heed her call;
And they who were evil-minded knew
Her nerve was strong and her aim was true.
So all kind words and acts did deal
To generous, black-eyed Jennie M'Neal.

One night, when the sun had crept to bed,
And rain-clouds lingered overhead,
And sent their surly drops for proof
To drum a tune on the cottage roof,
Close after a knock at the outer door,
There entered a dozen dragoons or more.
Their red coats, stained by the muddy road,
That they were British soldiers showed;
The captain his hostess bent to greet,
Saying, "Madam, please give us a bit to eat;

The Ride of Jennie M'Neal.

We will pay you well, and, if may be,
This bright-eyed girl for pouring our tea;
Then we must dash ten miles ahead,
To catch a rebel colonel abed.
He is visiting home, as doth appear;
We will make his pleasure cost him dear."
And they fell on the hasty supper with zeal,
Close-watched the while by Jennie M'Neal.

For the gray-haired colonel they hovered near,
Had been her true friend, kind and dear;
And oft, in her younger days, had he
Right proudly perched her upon his knee,
And told her stories many a one
Concerning the French war lately done.
And oft together the two friends were,
And many the arts he had taught to her;
She had hunted by his fatherly side,
He had shown her how to fence and ride;
And once had said, "The time may be,
Your skill and courage may stand by me."
So sorrow for him she could but feel,
Brave, grateful-hearted Jennie M'Neal.

With never a thought or a moment more,
Bare-headed she slipped from the cottage door,
Ran out where the horses were left to feed,
Unhitched and mountèd the captain's steed,
And down the hilly and rock-strewn way
She urged the fiery horse of gray.
Around her slender and cloakless form
Pattered and moaned the ceaseless storm;
Secure and tight, a gloveless hand
Grasped the reins with stern command;
And full and black her long hair streamed,
Whenever the ragged lightning gleamed.
And on she rushed for the colonel's weal,
Brave, lioness-hearted Jennie M'Neal.

Hark! from the hills, a moment mute,
Came a clatter of hoofs in hot pursuit;
And a cry from the foremost trooper said,
"Halt! or your blood be on your head!"
She heeded it not, and not in vain
She lashed the horse with the bridle-rein.
So into the night the gray horse strode;
His shoes hewed fire from the rocky road;

"SO INTO THE NIGHT THE GRAY HORSE STRODE."

And the high-born courage that never dies
Flashed from his rider's coal-black eyes.
The pebbles flew from the fearful race;
The rain-drops grasped at her glowing face.
"On, on, brave beast!" with loud appeal,
Cried eager, resolute Jennie M'Neal.

"Halt!" once more came the voice of dread;
"Halt! or your blood be on your head!"
Then, no one answering to the calls,
Sped after her a volley of balls.
They passed her in her rapid flight,
They screamed to her left, they screamed to her right;
But, rushing still o'er the slippery track,
She sent no token of answer back,
Except a silvery laughter-peal,
Brave, merry-hearted Jennie M'Neal.

So on she rushed, at her own good will,
Through wood and valley, o'er plain and hill;
The gray horse did his duty well,
Till all at once he stumbled and fell,

Himself escaping the nets of harm,
But flinging the girl with a broken arm.
Still undismayed by the numbing pain,
She clung to the horse's bridle-rein,
And gently bidding him to stand,
Petted him with her able hand;
Then sprung again to the saddle-bow,
And shouted, "One more trial now!"
As if ashamed of the heedless fall,
He gathered his strength once more for all,
And, galloping down a hill-side steep,
Gained on the troopers at every leap;
No more the high-bred steed did reel,
But ran his best for Jennie M'Neal.

They were a furlong behind, or more,
When the girl burst through the colonel's door,
Her poor arm helpless hanging with pain,
And she all drabbled and drenched with rain,
But her cheeks as red as fire-brands are,
And her eyes as bright as a blazing star,
And shouted, "Quick! be quick, I say!
They come! they come! Away! away!"

Then sunk on the rude white floor of deal,
Poor, brave, exhausted Jennie M'Neal.

The startled colonel sprung, and pressed
The wife and children to his breast,
And turned away from his fireside bright,
And glided into the stormy night;
Then soon and safely made his way
To where the patriot army lay.
But first he bent, in the dim fire-light,
And kissed the forehead broad and white,
And blessed the girl who had ridden so well
To keep him out of a prison-cell.
The girl roused up at the martial din,
Just as the troopers came rushing in,
And laughed, e'en in the midst of a moan,
Saying, "Good sirs, your bird has flown.
'Tis I who have scared him from his nest;
So deal with me now as you think best."
But the grand young captain bowed, and said,
"Never you hold a moment's dread.
Of womankind I must crown you queen;
So brave a girl I have never seen.

Wear this gold ring as your valor's due;
And when peace comes I will come for you."
But Jennie's face an arch smile wore,
As she said, "There's a lad in Putnam's corps,
Who told me the same, long time ago;
You two would never agree, I know.
I promised my love to be true as steel,"
Said good, sure-hearted Jennie M'Neal.

THREE SCENES OF A HERO'S LIFE.

I.

OLD Master Hobby, with a face
   Half serious, half grotesque,
And no one else within that place,
   Sat writing at his desk;

Conning long lessons, drear and sad,
   To make his boys rehearse;
Writing wise copies very bad,
   For them to copy worse.

Long, empty benches stretched around,
   And desks in stern array;
From boys outside there came a sound,
   Hard-working at their play.

When all at once a voice he heard:
  "You are the thief, not I!"
And back again the angry word
  Came, loud and clear, "You lie!"

Old Master Hobby left his seat:
  Across the dusty floor,
A pair of ragged-slippered feet
  His lean old body bore;

And putting up his wrinkled face
  (Unseen from out the yard),
Into a broken glass-pane's place,
  He watched and listened hard.

With fists tight-clenched, with feet firm-braced,
  Two boys stood, fast to fight;
Both savage-eyed and angry-faced,
  Shouting with all their might.

Old Master Hobby bent his brow
  And turned to seek the door,

As to himself he muttered, "Now,
   I'll whip the scamps full sore."

But at that moment came a voice—
   As if from one in doubt,
Crying above the tumult, "Boys,
   Why don't you leave it out?"

Then reason seemed to rule with one,
   And he at last replied,
"I'll leave it to George Washington,[8]
   To no one else beside."

Whereto the other did agree;
   When George appeared, and said,
"Since you have left it unto me,
   Thus to decide I'm led:

"Patrick, three pears, if true his claim,
   This boy has lost by you;
And from your somewhat blemished name,
   I rather think 'tis true.

"'SINCE YOU HAVE LEFT IT UNTO ME,
THUS TO DECIDE I'M LED.'"

"Your father has an orchard large;
    In payment for your tricks
Against your friend, I hereby charge
    That you shall pay him six.

"You, Nehemiah, here 'tis claimed,
    Your playmate's top have broke;
And, from the deeds for which you're famed,
    I fear 'tis truly spoke.

"Right easily your mind you bend
  The making toys to do;
So you the broken top shall mend,
  And give him one that's new."

At this the boys stood still a while,
  Thinking what should be done;
And the young umpire, with a smile,
  Was calmly looking on.

But rage again came surging through
  Each passion-heated head,
And both declared they would not do
  What had to them been said.

Whereat the young peace-maker cried,
  "You left the case to me;
I took pains justly to decide,
  From all that I could see.

"But you with heedless rage are mad,
  For foolish fight equipped;

And each would probably be glad
  To see the other whipped.

"So if you will not heed my plan,
  But both are bound to fight,
I'll whip you both—I think I can—
  And that will set it right."

The boys full well his bravery knew
  In every time of need;
And each stepped back a pace or two,
  And with the terms agreed.

The Master hobbled back, right glad
  His duties to rehearse,
And went to making copies bad,
  For them to copy worse;

And muttered to himself, "That one
  Of all my lads is best,
Who, when 'tis fitting to be done,
  Can govern all the rest.

"The boy who heard this childish cause,
    And when his mind was set,
Stood ready to enforce his laws,
    May rule a nation yet."

II.

MOTHER.

My boy, the hour is approaching I've dreaded long to know;
For out on the broad blue ocean the good ship waits to go.

All of your baggage safely upon its deck is stored;
Many a love-made token is safe for you on board.

Soon will your ears be greeted by the mariner's cheerful hail;
Soon on the wide, free ocean your gallant ship will sail.

Wonder not at the freedom with which I count my fears;
Do not let your courage be cowed by my rising tears;

Never from any other can my fond thoughts be heard;
Only a loving mother can speak a mother's word.

Long I with Heaven have pleaded your going not to see;
Long I my soul have flattered this cup would pass from me.

But there is naught can fetter a youth's adventurous joy;
Manhood's bravery sparkles in the heart of a healthy boy.

Yet as I think of the fair child I oft have cradled to sleep,
As tossed in the rude gale's dangers, as drenched by the savage deep,

Come to my heart forebodings that will not go their way;
Comes to my lips a yearning to plead you still to stay!

SON.

And true there are some dangers upon the merry sea;
And sure there are some death-gales, and one may come to me;

But Danger has its slumbers, and Safety smiles on care;
And boys soon grow to manhood, and men were made to dare.

Although you would do o'ermuch my life perchance to save,
Your love would melt to pity were I not strong and brave;
This moment your affection your high ambition hides;
I would have you love me, mother, and proud of me besides.

MOTHER.

But oft I have dreamed of a glory that waits to fall on you:
A glory of love and honor that shines for the brave and true.

You as a soldier-hero were o'er the earth renowned;
You by maids and matrons with laurel wreaths were crowned.

First in cold and darkness you crossed to a river-side,
Where to your brave endeavors was victory denied;

Next, in a blaze of sunshine 'neath skies of sweetest blue,
Maids and matrons waited with laurel wreaths for you.

Honors and praises added fresh beauty to your fame;
Heart-born blessings hovered about your noble name.

In no dream should aught be to turn you either way;
Still in my heart is a yearning to plead you still to stay!

SON.

And true a faithful soldier a valiant name may win;
But there are ports of honor that sailors enter in.
If for my brow a chaplet awaiting there may be,
Why can I not go find it upon the merry sea?

It is not *where* we struggle that we may win a name;
Upon both land and water true courage burns the same.

Though I may ne'er be famous, I'll mind my duty true;
And that is something noble for any one to do.

MOTHER.

Who can dispute a moment the truth of what you say?
Who can reject the logic with which you pave your way?

If on the scales of reason this question's truth be weighed,
Then is my cause defeated, and your decision made.

But there is something stronger by which my soul is stirred;
E'en when the brain speaks loudest, the heart will have its word.

Out of my love's bright garden the thorns of self-will grow:
And as the hour approaches, I will not let you go!

SON.

I care not for the dangers—I fear not for the pain;
I e'er have had a longing to live upon the main;

"'WEEP NOT, MY MORE THAN MOTHER; WASTE NOT A SINGLE TEAR.
I WILL NOT LEAVE YOU GRIEVING; I STILL WILL TARRY HERE.'"

But 'tis one thing to bear up against a farewell's smart,
And it is quite another to break a mother's heart.

Weep not, my more than mother; waste not a single tear.
I will not leave you grieving; I still will tarry here.

I would not bruise the warm arms that now my neck
    enfold,
To sail across the ocean a solid ship of gold.

III.

Sweetly down the Delaware
    Shone the smiling April sun;
Maids and matrons waited there
    For the honored Washington.[10]
Down the river's peaceful side
    Calm and stately he did ride;
On his proud and prancing steed,
He a hero looked indeed.
Voices loud on every hand
    Named him bravest of the brave,
Riding down to rule the land
    He had struggled there to save.

Where amid the wintry storm
   Long he fought through weary hours,
Now his tall and noble form
   Rode beneath an arch of flowers.
Many a blessing sweet and kind
In the tasteful wreaths was twined;
Many a kiss of purest love
Clustered in the bloom above:
And the words, with meaning fraught,
   Met his eyes, in golden hue,
"He who for the mothers fought
   Will protect the daughters, too."

Just before his steed's high head,
   Clad in robes of purest white,
Maidens marched, with reverent tread,
   Strewing flowers for his delight.
From beneath the welcome feet
Blessings flashed, his eyes to greet;
From above the stately head
Blessings fresh and true were shed;
From the eager watching throng
   Came the praise of great deeds done,

"JUST BEFORE HIS STEED'S HIGH HEAD,
CLAD IN ROBES OF PUREST WHITE,
MAIDENS MARCHED, WITH REVERENT TREAD,
STREWING FLOWERS FOR HIS DELIGHT."

UNIV. OF
CALIFORNIA

In the chorus loud and long,
   "Welcome, noble Washington!"

Could the mother but have gazed
   On the pageant-glittering stream,
She her heart to Heaven had raised,
   Full of thanks for that bright dream;
But the scene she would have eyed
With no look of pompous pride,
And the praise she would have heard
With no proud, exultant word;
But one prayer had struggled through,
   Fully answered yet to be;
"Make him to his country true,
   As he e'er has been to me."

THE PARENTS' FAREWELL.

FATHER.

SHOULDER arms, my good boy; never a minute pause;
Off to the patriot army, an' fight for your country's cause.
Though I be turned o' seventy, I'd go with you to-day,
Only upon a long march a crutch gets in the way.

Long I fought for England before she broke her trust;
I stood close by Braddock[11] the day he bit the dust.
Oft have I showed the Britishers that Yankees was no sham;
An' didn't I leave my right leg on the Plains of Abraham?[12]

Didn't I fight the Indians as well as a man could do?
Didn't they know for a certain that I was enough for two?
An' when I buried your brothers, with Indian bullets slain,
Could any body tell me I sought revenge in vain?

THE PARENTS' FAREWELL.

But now with sword an' musket there's nothing I can do;
My strength is all in the old time — my fighting days are through;
An' all I am lately good for is to sit by the chimney-jamb,
An' tell the boys how we whipped 'em on the Plains of Abraham.

I'd thought I might doze peaceful the evenin' of my
    days,
With you to wait upon me, with all your kindly ways;
But now the land of England I fought so faithful for
Is raising up against us the blood-red hand of war.

She's up an' dressed for conflict—she's comin' over here,
As if we couldn't keep house with none to interfere;
But we the sour old lady a piece of our mind will give,
And show her to the door-way, an' send her home to
    live.

And if there's scarce o' soldiers, you just sit down and
    write,
An' I'll come an' stop a bullet from some one who can
    fight;
An' if defeat awaitin' our army you may see,
Then do not mind my game leg, but hurry an' send for
    me.

MOTHER.

Four have to the death-shades gone
Of the five sons I have known:

One fell on a war-ship's deck,
One in sight of strong Quebec;
Two were dead before me laid
By the Indians' bloody blade;
One was struck down in his prime
By the hardships of the time,
And his manly heart lies still
'Neath the maples on the hill.
But the moments will not stay;
Shoulder arms, and march away!

Wait a moment yet, my son!
My heart's words are not yet done.
We are losing fast our hold—
We are feeble, bent, and old;
Wealth has never found our door—
We are helpless, weak, and poor.
But your arm, that was our stay;
Your bright smile, that cheered our way;
Your love, which the food has given
For which our poor hearts have striven,
We unto our country owe.
Shoulder arms, my boy, and go!

Young Folks' Centennial Rhymes.

Wait a minute! one word more!
I've so many thoughts in store!
May be in your childhood's year
We were somewhat too severe;
But for any word or blow
That we gave you long ago,
If it would have served the call,
We had rather they did fall
Wheresoever they were due—
On ourselves, and not on you.
But my poor old tongue is slow;
Shoulder arms, my boy, and go!

Wait! if e'er a hasty word
From our trembling lips you've heard,
Do not mind it when you're gone;
Let your love for us keep on.
Old folks' weakness, aches, an' pains
Oft are o'ermuch for their brains;
Old folks' sorrows, fear, and care
Are a load for them to bear.
You must due allowance make
In your memory for our sake.

The Parents' Farewell.

But my words too many grow;
Shoulder arms, my boy, and go!

One word more, and then adieu!
We had fondly hoped that you,
When we lay in death's repose,
Might be near, our eyes to close.
But 'tis overplain to see
How that joy may never be.
Ere your flag in victory waves,
We may sleep in lonely graves.
Nothing do, in toil or mirth,
That will grieve us, if on earth;
And if dead, perhaps our love
Will look on you from above;

So do nothing that if named
E'er need make you feel ashamed.
Either here, or else on high,
We shall meet you by-and-by;
Live so, when our forms you see,
Wheresoever it may be,

If victorious in your fight,
By our fireside warm and bright,
Or within a brighter place,
You can look us in the face.
But they need you 'gainst the foe;
Shoulder arms, my boy, and go!

HOW ISRAEL WAS WHIPPED.[13]

SCENE, BOSTON; TIME, 1730.

Enter ISRAEL, *a boy clad in country garb, and staring at every thing around him.*

ISRAEL.

WELL, if this don't beat all! I never knew
There were so many housen the whole world through.
Whichever way I look, a house I see;
They're thick as girls is, at a pearin'-bee.
I used to Salem town quite large allow,
But Salem ain't no object to me now.
Why, this 'ere town would never stop before
It ate ours up, an' smacked its lips for more!
And all these people, steppin' 'round here, too!
What under sun can they all find to do?

An' some of them are dressed as fine an' gay
As if there was a trainin' here to-day!

Enter a City Boy, *much larger than* ISRAEL, *and smartly dressed*.

CITY BOY.

What are you staring at, my tender one?
What are you looking for, my verdant son?

ISRAEL.

I'm starin' at whatever takes my eye;
I'm hunting for a gentleman.   Good-bye.

CITY BOY (*changing his manner*).

Why, I'm a gentleman, and I will do
My best to help you, if you want me to.
I know the city well; you, by your face,
Are but a stranger here.   Is this the case?

ISRAEL.

It ain't for me to rub out what you say;
I *am* a stranger, come from Salem way,

A-saltin' down such facts as I can see;
An' all these sights 'round here is news to me.

CITY BOY.

Is that a fact? We'll soon put *that* to rights;
I'll take you round, and show you all the sights.

ISRAEL.

Well, if you want to, all I've got to say,
Is, if you ever come out Salem way,
I'll take you to bring up, while you are there,
An' show you 'round, an' treat you good an' square.

CITY BOY.

All right, my rose; I'll put that promise down.
And now let's take a look about the town.
Perhaps you've heard it said, "out Salem way,"
The world turns on its axis once each day?

ISRAEL.

Well, yes; that's what last winter's school-ma'am said,
But hanged if I could get it through my head.

It was so mighty hard for me to see,
The woman had to whip it into me.

CITY BOY.

Well, it is true; although it moves so slow,
That, do your best, you can not *see* it go;
But ere he's here long every body learns,
This city is the place 'round which it turns.
You see that church-spire, just before your nose?
Well, that's the very point 'round which it goes.

ISRAEL.

You're sure, I hope (if 'twouldn't be impolite),
That this isn't something that you've dreamed some night?

CITY BOY.

Oh, yes! it's all dead truth, strange as may seem.
Why, bless your soul! I have no time to dream!
For if the truth is known—'cross, up, and down—
I own about three-quarters of this town.
You see those ships out yonder in the bay?
They all are mine; I build one every day.

ISRAEL.

It's getting late, and if you have not made
One for to-day, you'd best be at your trade.

CITY BOY.

Oh, I've a thousand men my work to do!
I send my ships to every country, too:
To Europe, Asia, Africa, they go;
I've lately put wings on them—do you know—
And sent them to the moon. When the wind's fair,
We Boston people get our cheese from there.

ISRAEL.

Now look ye here, my fine friend, if ye please:
Don't tell *me* that the moon is made o' cheese!
If that we find one blackbird in a nest,
We straightway kill for blackbirds all the rest;
So this last being any thing but true,
I rather think you've lied the whole way through.

CITY BOY (*angrily*).

You doubt my word, you green young country stick!
Well, then, I'll trounce you till I make you sick!

ISRAEL.

You've told a-many things I falsehoods guessed;
I b'lieve I doubt that more than all the rest.

BY-STANDER (*to* City Boy).

Stand back, you coward-lubber! don't you see,
You fool, that you are twice as big as he?

CITY BOY.

No; let him come an' touch me if he dar's!
I'll make him think the moon is made of stars!

> [*They fight;* ISRAEL *throws the* City Boy, *and holds him by the throat, the bystanders applauding.*

Pray let me up! I only was in fun!

ISRAEL.

An' I'm in earnest. Now, my pretty one,
You take that church-spire story back?

CITY BOY.

Oh yes!

ISRAEL.

You'll own you don't own Boston now, I guess?

CITY BOY.

Oh yes! that was a piece of nonsense too.
I'll give my city claims all up to you!

ISRAEL.

You own the moon ain't cheese?

CITY BOY.

Oh yes! oh, dear!

ISRAEL.

You'll own you are a liar, as you lie here?

CITY BOY.

Yes, yes! I own it all! Just let me go,
An' after this my tongue shall move more slow.

ISRAEL.

Then, take your feet, an' go upon your way,
An' be more truthful on another day.

An' when a country boy comes into town,
Don't try, first thing, to make him out a clown;
Use him as you'd be used; and, if you please,
Don't tell him that the moon is made of cheese.

LITTLE GOLDEN-HAIR.[1]

LITTLE GOLDEN-HAIR was watching, in the window broad and high,
  For the coming of her father, who had gone the foe to fight;
He had left her in the morning, and had told her not to cry,
  But to have a kiss all ready when he came to her at night.
      She had wondered, all the day,
      In her simple, childish way,
      And had asked, as time went on,
      Where her father could have gone;
She had heard the muskets firing, she had counted every one,
  Till the number grew so many that it was too great a load;

Then the evening fell upon her, clear of sound of shout or gun,
    And she gazed with wistful waiting down the dusty Concord road.

Little Golden-hair had listened, not a single week before,
    While the heavy sand was falling on her mother's coffin-lid:
And she loved her father better for the loss that then she bore,
    And thought of him, and yearned for him, whatever else she did.
        So she wondered all the day
        What could make her father stay,
        And she cried a little, too,
        As he'd told her not to do;
And the sun sunk slowly downward and went grandly out of sight,
    And she had the kiss all ready on his lips to be bestowed;
But the shadows made one shadow, and the twilight grew to night,
    And she looked, and looked, and listened, down the dusty Concord road.

Then the night grew light and lighter, and the moon rose full and round,
  In the little sad face peering, looking piteously and mild;
Still upon the walks of gravel there was heard no welcome sound,
  And no father came there, eager for the kisses of his child.

      Long and sadly did she wait,
      Listening at the cottage-gate;
      Then she felt a quick alarm,
      Lest he might have come to harm;

With no bonnet but her tresses, no companion but her fears,
  And no guide except the moonbeams that the pathway dimly showed,
With a little sob of sorrow, quick she threw away her tears,
  And alone she bravely started down the dusty Concord road.

And for many a mile she struggled, full of weariness and pain,
  Calling loudly for her father, that her voice he might not miss;

Till at last, among a number of the wounded and the slain,
  Was the white face of the soldier, waiting for his daughter's kiss.
        Softly to his lips she crept,
        Not to wake him as he slept;
        Then, with her young heart at rest,
        Laid her head upon his breast;
And upon the dead face smiling, with the living one near by,
  All the night a golden streamlet of the moonbeams gently flowed;
One to live, a lonely orphan, one beneath the sod to lie—
  They found them in the morning on the dusty Concord road.

THE PRIZE OF THE "MARGARETTA."[16]

I.

FOUR young men, of a Monday morn,
Heard that the flag of peace was torn;

Heard that "rebels," with sword and gun,
Had fought the British at Lexington,

While they were far from that bloody plain,
Safe on the green-clad shores of Maine.

With eyes that glittered, and hearts that burned,
They talked of the glory their friends had earned,

And asked each other, "What can we do,
So our hands may prove that our hearts are true?"

II.

Silent the *Margaretta* lay,
Out on the bosom of the bay;

On her masts rich bunting gleamed;
Bravely the flag of England streamed.

The young men gazed at the tempting prize—
They wistfully glanced in each other's eyes;

Said one, "We can lower that cloth of dread,
And hoist the pine-tree flag[16] instead.

"We are only boys to the old and sage;
We have not yet come to manhood's age;

"But we can show them that, when there's need,
Men may follow and boys may lead."

Tightly each other's hand they pressed,
Loudly they cried, "We will do our best;

"The pine-tree flag, ere day is passed,
Shall float from the *Margaretta's* mast."

III.

They ran to a sloop that lay near by;
They roused their neighbors, with hue and cry;

They doffed their hats, gave three loud cheers,
And called for a crew of volunteers.

Their bold, brave spirit spread far and wide,
And men came running from every side.

Curious armed were the dauntless ones,
With axes, pitchforks, scythes, and guns;

They shouted, "Ere yet this day be passed,
The pine-tree grows from the schooner's mast!"

IV.

With sails all set, trim as could be,
The *Margaretta* stood out to sea.

With every man and boy in place,
The gallant Yankee sloop gave chase.

Rippled and foamed the sunlit seas;
Freshened and sung the soft May breeze;

And came from the sloop's low deck, "Hurray!
We're gaining on her! We'll win the day!"

A sound of thunder, echoing wide,
Came from the *Margaretta's* side;

A deadly crash, and a loud death-yell,
And one of the brave pursuers fell.

They aimed a gun at the schooner then,
And sent the compliment back again;

He who at the helm of the schooner stood,
Covered the deck with his rich life-blood.

v.

Each burning to pay a bloody debt,
The crews of the hostile vessels met;

The Western nation now to be,
Made her first fight upon the sea.

And not till forty men were slain,
Did the pine-tree flag a victory gain;

But at last the hearts of the Britons quailed,
And grandly the patriot arm prevailed.

One of the youths, the deed to crown,
Grasped the colors and pulled them down;

And raised, 'mid cries of wild delight,
The pine-tree flag of blue and white.

And the truth was shown, for the world to read,
That men may follow and boys may lead.

THE PRINTER-BOY TRAMP."

Oh, mother! come and see this lad, a-loitering down the street!
As queer a looking one he is as one would want to meet.
His face is full of thought and dirt—his brow's a savage scowl;
He has a wise expression on, as solemn as an owl.
His hair has not been combed to-day—that's easy understood;
But there's something in his eye, mother, that's sensible and good.

His clothes are somewhat patched and torn—his hat's the worse for wear,
He perches it upon his head with very little care;
His shoes are rough, and bear the marks of many a dusty mile;
He's any thing but a success, considered for his style.

He has a monster of a foot — a large and sun-browned hand—
But there's something in his air, mother, like one born to command.

Look! As he walks along the street, with proud, indifferent tread,
Close underneath each of his arms he hugs a loaf of bread!
He does not mind the difference 'twixt a dining-room and street,
But from a loaf that's in his hand continues still to eat.
The boys they wink and laugh at him; the people smile and stare;
But there's something in his way, mother, that says he does not care.

He's walked away; but, strange to say, he still runs in my head;
I still can see him, in my mind, with his three loaves of bread.

I know he is no common lad—of course, it's all the same;
How awkward and how rude he was!—I wish I knew his name.
Of course, I do not care for him, so shabby and so queer;
But there's something in my heart, mother, that wishes he were here.

Nellie's Lie.

NELLIE'S LIE.

As Nellie 'neath the oak-tree sat and sewed,
There came a Hessian¹ⁿ soldier up the road;
His arm was red, where blood from it had flowed.

Panting, he walked up at a feeble pace,
He looked the little girl straight in the face,
And said, "Please give to me a hiding-place!

"From death-hounds, close pursuing me, I fly;
Five of my foemen swift are coming nigh,
And if they find me, I must surely die.

"I have a little girl across the sea,
About your size, and she is fond of me,
As you of your own father sure must be.

"She has a heart as tender as 'tis true;
If now to her *your* father, wounded, flew,
I know that she would do as much for you.

"Perhaps, to-day, while I from danger flee,
By our small cottage, far across the sea,
Poor Gretchen weeps, and vainly waits for me."

And Nellie paused; it was her father's foe;
But could she turn away and bid him go,
Bleeding and weak, to meet a mortal blow?

And still she paused, and pity fought with fear;
She heard the tramp of soldiers coming near—
She pointed to the tree, and whispered, "Here!

"Within these branches, safe the leaves amid,
From all my playmates I have often hid;
Climb up, and do not come till you are bid!"

* * * * * * *

"SHE BOUND HIS ARM."

The soldiers dashed up, saying, "You must know,
We chase to-day a bloody Hessian foe;
We think you must have seen him; is it so?"

She blushed—she pondered what was wrong or right—
Then looked up, with her great eyes sparkling bright,
And answered, "Yes; he just went out of sight."

"Did he go up, or down, or straight ahead?"
Pointing, meanwhile, to where a cross-road led;
"Up," Nellie, at her sewing, faintly said.

Right onward still swept the pursuing band;
The Hessian came down at the girl's command;
He humbly kissed his young preserver's hand.

She bound his arm—he bade her not to fear;
She gave him food—he brushed away a tear;
She said "Good-bye"—he sought the forest near.

She thought, "Perhaps 'twas not to country true,
But 'twas what I would have *his* girl to do;
And Gretchen—wouldn't she thank me, if she knew!"

DICEY LANGSTON.[19]

SCENE, MR. LANGSTON'S HOUSE, IN LAURENS DISTRICT, SOUTH CAROLINA; TIME, NIGHT.

MRS. LANGSTON.

Hark! what's that noise?

MR. LANGSTON.

Nothing, except the wind
Flying among the trees.

MRS. LANGSTON.

But what is that?

MR. LANGSTON.

Some rabbit, or some fox, that prowls outside,
Seeking for food or shelter.

MRS. LANGSTON.

      And what's that?

MR. LANGSTON.

An owl—bird-watch-dog of the woods: he makes
The night seem twice as lonely.

MRS. LANGSTON.

      Oh, my child!
Rushing through dangers, creeping over snares,
For three long days and nights you have been
 gone,
And I a-sitting safely here at home!
Why did I let you go upon this journey?

MR. LANGSTON.

To save your other children.

MRS. LANGSTON.

      And, perhaps,
Lose them the same, and her besides. 'Tis sad
To sit here childless, may be, and reflect
That she to-night might be here safe with me,

If I had not surrendered to her pleading!
What's that?

MR. LANGSTON.

A step.

MRS. LANGSTON.

A voice! *Her* voice, thank God!

Enter DICEY.

DICEY.

Home again, safe! Oh, 'twas an awful tramp!
Why, father, how you hug me! And you, mother,
Are crying so, it brings tears to my eyes.
Why, one would think I had been gone a year,
And then the word had come that I was dead,
Instead of being absent three short days,
And then returning safely home to you.

MRS. LANGSTON.

Three days and nights! You must be starved to
death!

DICEY.

Oh no! not near! 'Tis not so easy done!
Two things are o'erhard with a healthy girl:
Those are, to starve her, and to break her heart.

MR. LANGSTON.

You must be tired to death with lack of sleep.

DICEY.

Oh no! I slept to-day in the safe house
Of one who stands within her door, and shouts,
"Long live our great and glorious George the Third!"
But whispers to her girls, "Get supper, now,
For the next rebel who may come along."
She hides the patriot colors in a trunk,
And when there's news of rebel victories,
She drapes her bedroom with our country's flag,
Shuts the doors tight, that none outside may hear,
And shouts, "Hurra for Washington and right!"

MRS. LANGSTON.

Now you are safe, dear daughter, what about
The ones you went to save? Were you in time?

DICEY.

Yes, in full time! Let me alone for that!
And the red Cunningham will have to scent
Farther than he has ever done before,
If he makes good his threat of finding them.
Let him look out they are not finding him!
For they are rallying swift to give him fight.

MR. LANGSTON.

Your journey must have been a rough one, girl.

DICEY.

'Twas not a pleasure trip, I must confess.
It was a long and fearful walk. The night
I left my home, the storms were quarreling;
And as I felt along the hard-found path,
Great clouds seemed e'en a'most to brush my head.
Cold drops plashed in my face; the wind sometimes
Made such a doleful sound, it almost seemed
That 'twas some dead man, waked up in his grave.
Once, at first sight, I thought I saw a ghost,
That beckoned to me with its long white arms,
As if to call me to it; then I shouted,

"Say! If you are an honest rebel ghost,
Come and shake hands; if not, go on your way,
And let an honest girl go hers in peace."

MRS. LANGSTON.

Why, Dicey! How could you dare be so bold?

DICEY.

What is a ghost, for any one to fear?
Are ghosts good eaters? Would they eat me up?
I do not think there ever was a ghost.
But if there are such things, they're not so fierce
That any one need fear them. Now, when I
Am not afraid of any man *alive*,
Tell me, why should I fear him when he's *dead?*
Ghosts may have arms; but have they flesh on them?
They may have mouths; but have they teeth in them?
They're cowards, too, and ne'er can stand their ground,
If you will talk good honest sense to them.
I'd rather that a thousand ghosts would come,
And grin about me with their faces white,
And beckon to me with their long thin arms,
Than have a live wolf growl too close to me.

MR. LANGSTON.

You wouldn't run for the wolf; but, I'll be bound,
'Twas not a ghost. Go on and tell the rest
About your journey. We are fast to hear.

DICEY.

Well, when I started for it, and cried out,
It disappeared, as ghosts will always do;
I think my fancy must have made it all.
Just then I stumbled on some little thing,
That gave a cry of anguish; and I stooped
And picked it up; it was a little bird;
And it had lost its nest, and helpless lay,
With none to care for it. I picked it up,
And said, "*My poor, weak, helpless, silly thing!*
This is a cold world into which you've come,
Thinking, perhaps, that you can live in it;
But here you are, just ready now to die.
Say! is it war-time, too, among the birds,
That you are here so helpless and so lone,
Without a mother nigh to care for you?
Perhaps the great God—who has said that He
Would never see a sparrow fall without

Noting just where it lay—has picked me out
To save your life; so come with me, my dear."
It nestled trustingly into my hand;
And so I carried it unto the end
Of my long journey, and protected it
Even when dangers hung above my head.
I left it safe with friends, and made them say,
That when 'twas strong they'd give its freedom
    back.

MR. LANGSTON.

Well, that was noble, good, and kind in you,
And, mayhap, interesting—to the bird;
But we had rather hear what 'came of you.

DICEY.

Trudging along the road, I heard a sound
Like horses' hoof-steps; so I drew one side,
And hid myself behind a wayside tree,
More like some rogue than a well-meaning girl
Struggling to save the lives of them she loved.
It was a company of British horse;
And as they galloped past, I heard them drone,

"*God save the King!*" 'Twas all that I could do,
To keep from shouting, so that they could hear,
"*And take him into heaven this very night!*"

MRS. LANGSTON.

Dicey, you must not wish that folks would die.

DICEY.

I know 'twas wicked; but it seemed, somehow,
As if the thought would come, in spite of me.

MR. LANGSTON.

Tell your adventures; let your politics
Go till another time.

DICEY.

                Your pardon, father.
Well, on I walked, through midnight cold and black;
And, just before the morning streaked the east,
Came to the river's ford. The waters raged,
Swollen by the rains, and all was drear and dark.
What should I do? I stood there for a while,
Thinking what I should do: behind me, home

And parents, needing my good watch and care;
Before me was my duty; but, perhaps,
Death in between us. For a while I stood;
Then, with a stern resolve to do my best,
And a short prayer, I stepped into the stream.
The water touched my knees—my waist—my arms;
I felt a shudder as the cold chills struck
Through me; and still the water crept and crept,
Up to my shoulders—to my chin—my mouth;
And still I prayed for guidance, and pressed on.
Which way I went, or up or down the stream,
Or whether for the shore—I did not know;
I only prayed, and struggled on. And once
The water swept up past my mouth; and then
I strangled, but kept on; when, in a trice,
It grew less deep—less deep—less deep—and then
I came out on the bank, and found the road,
And once more went my way, drenched to the skin,
And cold, and chilled, and clogged with clinging
    drops;
But my heart felt so warm, it almost seemed
As if 'twould dry me in a little time.
The morning got there just before me. When

I knocked at brother's door, he did not know
What evil beast so early was abroad,
And near had shot me for an enemy. But when
I gave my message, and they knew what risk,
What labor, and what pain I had endured
To save their lives, they gave me such a cheer!

MRS. LANGSTON.

Thank Heaven you're safe! Thank Heaven your
    brothers are!

MR. LANGSTON.

And give the girl some credit, too. Now what!
    [*A knock at the door. Enter the bloody* Scouts.

CUNNINGHAM.

Your rebel sons came very near their death,
Old man. A little more, and we had found
Their hiding-place; but they had run away.
The Lord knows how they scented us so soon!

DICEY (*aside*).

And I know, too.

MR. LANGSTON.

Thank God!

SECOND SCOUT.

Old rebel!

THIRD SCOUT.

Kill him!

[*Second Scout points his gun at* MR. LANG-
STON; DICEY *throws herself between them.*

DICEY.

I am the cause of all your trouble, sirs;
I traveled through the midnight, and alarmed
My brothers to their danger. If you kill,
Kill me. I am the one. What! Harm my father?
Him whose gray head has not a sinful hair?
Shoot, soldiers! shoot! and kill a weak, pale girl!
For now I swear no bullet shall go nigh
His body, but it first shall crash through mine!

CUNNINGHAM.

Well, that's well acted.

DICEY.

And well meant.

CUNNINGHAM.

Oh, well,
If you'll be taking on at such a pitch,
We'll let you go this time, and go ourselves.
No doubt, my little shrew, you'll yet get hung;
For you're the liveliest rebel in the State.
But 'twill be sin to hurt so brave a girl!
Forward, march!

[*They pass out.*

MRS. LANGSTON.

Good, brave daughter! it is you
Have saved your brothers' lives, and now your father's!

DICEY.

I did no more than what I felt, dear mother.
I've heard that you were glad, when I was born,
A daughter had at last come here to you;
But father thought 'twas hard, in such fierce times,

In these wild woods, that all could not be sons.
I often heard this whispered, when I 'came
So old that I could understand it; then
I vowed that I would be as useful to
The father that I loved as any son.

MR. LANGSTON.

And well you've kept your vow. And if, indeed,
It is a sin to be a girl, you yet
Right well have made it up. But did you see
Young Springfield in the settlement? Ah, now
You blush.

DICEY (*coloring*).

He was not there. What's he to me?

MR. LANGSTON.

More than you'll own, my girl. You have the heart
Of woman, with the courage of a man.
  [*Another knock at the door. Enter* three Men, *disguised*.

FIRST MAN.

Is this the house of Mister Langston?

MR. LANGSTON.

          Yes.

FIRST MAN.

We are three patriot soldiers, watching sharp
For that bold captain, the red Cunningham.

MR. LANGSTON.

Then follow quick, if you'd be finding him;
Or run quick, if you fear he will find you;
For he is not a half a mile away.

SECOND MAN.

We fly from him! Not now! Our force is large,
And we shall capture him before the morn.
But we were told, sir, by your oldest son,
To call here for a gun that he had left.

MR. LANGSTON.

Dicey, go bring it.

DICEY (*appearing with it*).

      Here it is, sir. Oh!
There is a pass-word must be had for this;

My brother said I should not give it up
Without the pass-word.

SECOND MAN.

But, my pretty miss,
Why should we need to give a pass-word now?
We have you all here in our power; the gun
Is ours already.

DICEY (*cocking the gun, and pointing it at him*).

Yours already? Well,
If it is yours, take charge of it!

THIRD MAN.

Hold! hold!
Don't fire, my girl! I'll give the countersign.
"Death to the tyrant! Liberty and right!"

DICEY (*trembling and blushing, and giving up the gun*).
I know that voice! 'Tis Thomas Springfield!

SPRINGFIELD.

Yes;
I have just come from Marion. He has heard

Of your adventures, and has sent this ring,
From his own finger, as an offering
And testimonial to your bravery.

[*Aside to* DICEY.

And as for me, I have another ring,
Which I would place upon your finger, if—

DICEY (*aside to him*).

Never, until my country's wars are done,
Will I accept the hand of any one.
Whatever love or loves may plead with me,
My country is my love till she be free.

SPRINGFIELD.

And if I'm faithful—when the war is done,
And by my help our freedom has been won—

DICEY (*giving him her hand*).

Then come to me, and claim my heart's reply.

SPRINGFIELD.

I will remind you of these words.   Good-bye.

[Men *march out.*

NOTES.

NOTES.

[1] The name of "the little black-eyed rebel" was Mary Redmond. She was the daughter of a patriot who lived in Philadelphia at the time it was occupied by the British troops. In that city, and at the above-mentioned time, the incident told in the poem took place. The following account of the young heroine is taken from "Noble Deeds of American Women:"

"She had many relatives who were Loyalists, and these used to call her 'the little black-eyed rebel,' so ready was she to help women whose husbands were fighting for freedom in getting letters from them. The letters were usually sent from their friends by a boy, who carried them stitched in the back of his coat. He came into the city, bringing provisions to market. One morning, when there was some reason to fear he was suspected, and his movements were watched by the enemy, Mary undertook to get the papers from him in safety. She went as usual to the market, and, in a pretended game of romps, threw her shawl over the boy's head, and secured the prize. She hurried with the papers to her anxious friends, who read them secretly, after the windows had been carefully closed.

"When the news came that the British general, Burgoyne, had surrendered, the cunning little 'rebel,' so as not to be heard by her Loyalist friends, put her head up the chimney, and gave a shout for Gates, the American general."

[2] General Thomas Gage, who is here referred to, was British Governor of Massachusetts in the winter of 1774-'75, when this incident took place. He is said to have been a good-natured, sociable man; but he did not succeed as a governor, and was removed in 1775.

[3] On the morning of the attack upon the Sammons family, Thomas, the youngest, had risen earlier than usual, to feed his horses and go over to another farm near-by, to work with his brother. Just as he stepped out-of-doors, a hand was laid upon his shoulder, with the words, "You are my prisoner." So still had the enemy approached, that not the sound of a footstep was heard until that moment. By this time, the house was surrounded by the Tories. One of the officers, with several soldiers, then entered, and ordered the family to get up and surrender themselves as prisoners. Jacob and Frederick, who were in the second story, sprung up on their feet immediately, and seized their arms. The officer called to them, and told them they should not be hurt if they would surrender. Jacob inquired whether there were any Indians among them, adding that, if there were, they would not be taken alive. On being told there were none, they came down-stairs and surrendered. Old Mr. Sammons, also, was taken. They were ordered to get ready to march immediately, the British intending to take them to Canada as prisoners; but Thomas told the sentinel that he could not go so far without his shoes, which he

had not yet put on, and which he asked permission to get from upstairs. The soldier refused; Thomas sprung for the ladder, determined to get his shoes. The soldier made a plunge at his back with his bayonet, which would have killed the boy if it had not been for his sister, who sprung forward, and, seizing the gun, threw herself across the barrel, and, by falling, brought it to the ground. The soldier struggled to pull away the gun and accomplish his purpose; but an officer stepped up, and inquired what was the matter. The girl informed him, whereupon he ordered the man to step back, and let the boy get any thing he wanted for the journey.—*Life of General Brant.*

Thomas Sammons escaped that afternoon. When he became a man, he was elected a member of Congress for several years. Old Mr. Sammons was released on the same day he was captured; and the other two sons afterward escaped, and returned safely home.

[4] Paul Revere was the man who rode through the darkness, on the night of the 18th of April, 1775, to rouse the people, and tell them that the British were coming for the purpose of destroying the American military stores at Concord. An account of the incident may be found in Longfellow's splendid poem, "Paul Revere's Ride."

[5] "Sheridan's Ride" is a fine poem, by T. B. Read, relating the incident of General Sheridan's riding twenty miles from Winchester, to save the day in a battle.

[6] "The Neutral Ground" was so called in the Revolution, because it

was held by neither the American nor the British army, but lay between them. It was in Westchester County, New York. The people of this section had a hard time during the war; for they were liable at any moment to be robbed by friends of either of the armies, or by villains who cared nothing for the results of the conflict, but served all alike.

[7] Not long after the birth of George Washington, his father removed to an estate in Stafford County, opposite Fredericksburg. The house stood on a rising ground overlooking a meadow which bordered the Rappahannock River. This was the home of George's boyhood; the meadow was his playground and the scene of his early sports. But this home, like that in which he was born, has disappeared; the site is only to be traced by fragments of bricks, china, and earthenware.

George was yet in early childhood. As his intellect dawned, he received the rudiments of education in the best establishment for the purpose that the neighborhood afforded. It was what was called an "old field school-house," kept by one of his father's tenants, named Hobby, who was also sexton of the parish.—IRVING'S *Life of Washington*.

[8] Washington, when at old Master Hobby's school, was so well liked by his playmates, and they had so much confidence in his judgment and honesty, that when they fell into any trouble among themselves they very often called on him to act as judge, and to decide how the affair should be settled.

[9] When Washington was fourteen years of age, he had a great desire to

enter the British navy. It was necessary, however, to first get the consent of his mother, his father having died when he was eleven years old. After a great deal of urging, she consented to let him go; and his brother obtained for him the position of midshipman on a vessel of war, which, at that time, was anchored in the Potomac River, just below Mount Vernon. His baggage was all on board the ship, and he came to his mother to bid her good-bye; but at the last moment her heart failed her, and she took back her words of consent, and begged of him not to go. Rather than grieve her so sadly, he gave up his plan, had his baggage brought back to the house, and staid at home. Had he entered upon a sailor's life, he might never have become the leading general of the American Revolution.

[10] After the War of the Revolution was over, and the Americans had gained their independence, the question arose, Who should be the first President? Washington was elected to the place, and, much against his wishes, consented to serve. When peace was declared, he had gone back to his home at Mount Vernon, on the Potomac River, and hoped to spend the rest of his life there, quietly and easily, as a farmer. But the country would not consent to that; and, on the 16th of April, 1789, he started for Philadelphia, which was then the capital of the United States, to be inaugurated as President. His way took him through Trenton, New Jersey, where, a number of years before, he had spent a gloomy night, trying to outwit the British general, Cornwallis, and had succeeded in doing so. On a bridge, crossing the stream which flows through that city, the ladies had raised an arch, twined with evergreens and laurels, under which he was

to pass. Upon it were the words, "The defenders of the mothers will be the protectors of the daughters." A number of young girls, dressed in white, marched before him, and strewed flowers, singing, meanwhile, a song in his praise. The day was clear; the sun shone brightly; crowds of happy people were present; and Washington could not help noticing and feeling the difference between this beautiful day and the gloomy night he had spent upon the same river with his little army, twelve years before.

[11] General Edward Braddock was commander of the British and Americans, when they together were fighting the French, in the "French War," which took place a few years before the Revolution. This, of course, was while our forefathers were still under the power and protection of England. On the 9th of July, 1755, General Braddock marched, with a force of two thousand men, British and Americans, against Fort Du Quesne, now Pittsburgh, Pennsylvania, which was held by the French. On the way there, a band of French and Indians suddenly sprung out of the forest, and, after a severe fight, General Braddock's army was beaten, and ran away in disorder. After having five horses shot under him, the general was wounded, and died a few days after.

[12] "The Plains of Abraham" are near the city of Quebec, on the St. Lawrence River. Here, in 1769, the British army defeated the French, and took the city.

[13] "Israel," in the short scene, "How Israel was Whipped," refers to the boy who afterward became General Putnam, one of the bravest and

most faithful commanders in the American army. The following brief mention of his boyhood is gathered from Sparks's "Life of Putnam:"

He was born at Salem, in Massachusetts, on the 7th day of January, 1718. His grandfather, with two brothers, came from the South of England. His father was a farmer, and the son was brought up to the same pursuit, for which not much education was then believed to be needed. The arts of reading, writing, and a little of arithmetic were all that could be acquired in the common schools; so that the literary advantages of young Israel could not have been very great. But his body was firm and strong, and he was not afraid of any ordinary danger. It was the custom for young men in those days to practice running, leaping, wrestling, and pitching the bar; and in these manly sports Putnam could be beaten by none of his companions. On his first visit to Boston, he was treated rudely by one of the city boys, a sort of welcome which country boys frequently receive when they "go to town." His antagonist was twice as large as himself; but Israel gave him a sound beating, to the entire satisfaction of a large number who were looking on.

[14] The incident told in the poem, "Little Golden-hair," is supposed to have taken place when the British marched to destroy the American military stores at Concord, on the 18th of April, 1775. Upon this day occurred the first battle of the Revolution.

[15] The capture of the *Margaretta* took place near Machias, Maine, soon after the battle of Lexington. Mr. Lossing, in his "Field-book of the Revolution," says:

"The honor of this enterprise belongs to Joseph Wheaton, a native of New York, then residing at Machias. He was an energetic young man of twenty years. He proposed the expedition, but modestly named Jeremiah O'Brien for commander. He was active in the whole affair, and in person seized the colors of the *Margaretta*."

[16] "The Pine-tree Flag" was used upon American vessels, before the introduction of the "Stars and Stripes." It was white, with a picture of a pine-tree in the centre, and the words, "In God we Trust."

[17] "The Printer-boy Tramp" was Benjamin Franklin, who afterward became one of the greatest philosophers and statesmen of his time, and one of the most faithful patriots of the Revolution. When a boy, he paid his first visit to Philadelphia, in search of work, as a printer, which trade he had learned. His best clothes were in his trunk, which had not yet arrived; he had only a single dollar in his pocket; but he was not discouraged, and set about finding employment as soon as possible. Feeling hungry, he stepped into a baker's shop, and bought three large loaves of bread. With a loaf under each arm, and one in his hand, he proceeded up the street, eating his breakfast on the way, and never noticing the queer glances that followed him.

As he passed the house of Mr. Read, the daughter of Mr. R. was standing at the door, and is supposed to have said the words in the poem. She afterward became the wife of Franklin.

[18] The Hessians were soldiers whom the King of England had bought

or hired from a German prince, paying him a certain sum of money for each man. They were brought over the sea to fight the Americans. In order to get enough of them to fill out the number bargained for, the German prince sent his soldiers into fields and shops where the men were working, and into churches where they were worshiping, seized, and hurried them off, without giving them time even to say good-bye to their families. The Hessians were, many of them, more to be pitied than blamed.

[19] Dicey Langston was the daughter of Solomon Langston, of Laurens District, South Carolina. She possessed a brave spirit, which, living in the days of the Revolution, she had more than one chance to display. Situated in the midst of Tories, and being patriotically inquisitive, she often learned by accident, or discovered by strategy, the plottings so common in those days against the American patriots. This intelligence she used to communicate to the friends of freedom on the opposite side of the Ennoree River.

Learning one time that a band of the enemy, called the "Bloody Scouts," were about to fall on the "Elder Settlement," a place where brothers and other friends of hers were residing, she made up her mind to warn them of their danger. To do this, she must hazard her own life; but off she started, alone, in the darkness of the night, traveled several miles through the woods and over marshes and across creeks, through a country where foot-logs and bridges were then unknown; came to the Tyger, a deep stream, into which she plunged and waded till the water was up to her neck. She then became bewildered, and zigzagged the channel some time; but at length reached the opposite shore, for a helping hand was beneath, and a kind Providence guided her. She hastened on, reached the settlement, and her brothers and the whole community were safe.

She was returning one day from another settlement of patriots, when a company of Tories met her, and questioned her in regard to the neighborhood she had just left; but she refused to give them any information. The leader of the band then held a pistol to her breast, and threatened to shoot her, if she did not make the wished-for disclosure. "Shoot me, if you dare! I will not tell you!" she replied. The rascal, enraged at her obstinacy, was in the act of firing; but one of the soldiers threw up the hand holding the weapon, and the brave heart of the girl was permitted to beat on.

The brothers of Dicey were no less patriotic than she; and they having, by their active services in the cause of liberty, greatly displeased the enemy, the latter were determined to be revenged. A desperate band accordingly went to the house of their father, and, finding the sons absent, they were about to take their vengeance on the old man, whom they hated on account of his sons. With this intent, one of the party drew a pistol; but just as it was aimed at the breast of her aged and infirm father, Dicey rushed between the two, and, though the ruffian bid her get out of the way or take the contents of the weapon in her own breast, she flung her arms around her father's neck, and declared she would receive the ball first, if the pistol were fired. The heart of the "Bloody Scout" was softened, and Mr. Langston lived to see his noble daughter perform other heroic deeds.

One time, her brother James, in his absence, sent to the house for a gun which he had left in her care, with orders to deliver it to no one except by his direction. On reaching the house, one of the company made known the errand, whereupon she brought the gun, and was about to deliver it. At this moment it occurred to her that she had not demanded the pass-word agreed upon between herself and her brother. With the gun still in her hand, she looked the company sternly in the face, and called for the countersign. One of the company, for a joke, told her that she was too late; that the gun as well as the holder was already in their possession. "Do you think so?" she boldly asked, aiming it at him. "Then take charge of it!" Her appearance indicated that she was in earnest, and the pass-word was given without delay. A hearty laugh on the part of the "Liberty Men" ended the ceremony.—*Noble Deeds of American Women.*

Miss Langston married Thomas Springfield, of Greenville, South Carolina, where many of her descendants are still living.— LOSSING'S *Field-book of the Revolution.*

THE END.

www.ingramcontent.com/pod-product-compliance
Lightning Source LLC
Chambersburg PA
CBHW031409160426
43196CB00007B/960